AMERICA'S FAVORITE SYMBOLS

THE U.S. FLAG
STARS AND STRIPES FOREVER

JINNOW KHALID

New York

Published in 2021 by The Rosen Publishing Group, Inc.
29 East 21st Street, New York, NY 10010

First Edition

Portions of this work were originally authored by Walter LaPlante and published as *The US Flag*. All new material in this edition authored by Jinnow Khalid.

Editor: Elizabeth Krajnik
Book Design: Reann Nye

Photo Credits: Cover, p.1 Sergey Kamshylin/Shutterstock.com; Series Art sunwart/Shutterstock.com; p. 5 Susan Montgomery/Shutterstock.com; p. 7 Bill Chizek/Shutterstock.com; p. 9 (flag) https://commons.wikimedia.org/wiki/File:Hopkinson_Flag.svg; p. 9 (Hopkinson) mashuk/DigitalVision Vectors/Getty Images; p. 11 Robert Pernell/Shutterstock.com; p. 13 Wally Stemberger/Shutterstock.com; p. 15 Dmitri Kessel/The LIFE Images Collection/Getty Images; pp. 17, 19 Bettmann/Getty Images; p. 21 KieferPix/Shutterstock.com.

Library of Congress Cataloging-in-Publication Data

Names: Khalid, Jinnow, author.
Title: The U.S. flag : stars and stripes forever / Jinnow Khalid.
Description: New York : PowerKids Press, [2021] | Series: America's favorite symbols | Includes index.
Identifiers: LCCN 2019050882 | ISBN 9781725317390 (paperback) | ISBN 9781725317413 (library binding) | ISBN 9781725317406 (6 pack)
Subjects: LCSH: Flags–United States–History–Juvenile literature.
Classification: LCC CR113 .K48 2021 | DDC 929.9/20973–dc23
LC record available at https://lccn.loc.gov/2019050882

Manufactured in the United States of America

CPSIA Compliance Information: Batch #CSPK20. For Further Information contact Rosen Publishing, New York, New York at 1-800-237-9932.

CONTENTS

Meaningful Flag

The U.S. flag is one of the most common **symbols** of American pride. You probably see this flag every day. Each part of the flag has meaning. Today, the flag symbolizes many things to many people.

The Continental Colors

During the **American Revolution**, the colonies flew a flag called the **Continental** Colors. This flag had the first flag of Great Britain in the canton, or the top inner quarter of the flag. It also had 13 stripes.

The Stars and Stripes

On June 14, 1777, the Continental Congress chose the first **official** national flag, which is often called the Stars and Stripes. This flag had 13 stars on a blue field and 13 red and white stripes. Francis Hopkinson, a congressman from New Jersey, most likely created this flag.

Francis Hopkinson

Hopkinson's Flag

A Growing Country

The 13 stars and 13 stripes on the flag stood for the 13 colonies that became the first states in the United States. As the country continued to grow, a star was added to the flag's blue field whenever a new state joined the country.

At first, Congress added stripes for new states, too. After Vermont and Kentucky joined the country in the early 1790s, there were 15 stripes on the flag. However, in 1818, Congress passed a law that set the flag's stripes at 13.

Many Flags!

The law also said that each new star would be added to the flag on the July 4 following that state's addition. Between 1777 and 1960, there were 27 different U.S. flags. During that time, the stars were laid out in many different ways.

Standardizing the Flag

In 1912, President William Howard Taft signed a law that **standardized** the flag's size and the sizes of the stars and stripes. That flag had six side-to-side rows of eight stars each. Today's flag has 50 stars. It hasn't changed since 1960.

Symbolic Colors

The colors of the U.S. flag date back to the years of the Continental Congress and the creation of a **seal** for the new country. White stands for **purity**, red stands for bravery, and blue stands for fairness and truth.

E PLURIBUS
UNUM

Flag Day

Since 1916, Americans have **celebrated** Flag Day. This day honors the day the Continental Congress chose the first official national flag of the United States. People also honor the U.S. flag with songs, books, art, and much more!

Timeline

1777
The Continental Congress chooses the first official national flag, often called the Stars and Stripes.

1795
Congress adds two new stars and stripes to the flag to stand for Vermont and Kentucky.

1818
Congress passes a law setting the flag's stripes at 13 and the number of stars as equal to the number of states.

1912
President William Howard Taft signs a law that standardizes the flag's size and the sizes of the stars and stripes.

1916
President Woodrow Wilson creates Flag Day.

GLOSSARY

American Revolution: The war of 1775–1783 in which 13 British colonies in North America broke free from British rule and became the United States of America.

celebrate: To do something special or enjoyable for an important event, occasion, holiday, etc.

continental: Being the mainland part of a country, such as the part of the United States on the North American continent.

official: Done in a public and often formal way.

purity: Freedom from sin or guilt.

seal: An official mark stamped or pressed on something.

standardize: To make alike or matching a model.

symbol: Something that stands for something else.

INDEX

WEBSITES

Due to the changing nature of Internet links, PowerKids Press has developed an online list of websites related to the subject of this book. This site is updated regularly. Please use this link to access the list: www.powerkidslinks.com/afs/usflag